9. 95

Teen Pregnancy

Teen Pregnancy

by Sonia Bowe-Gutman

Lerner Publications Company
Minneapolis

Cover art by Jeffrey Kyle
Illustrations by Donald Stewart

Library of Congress Cataloging-in-Publication Data

Bowe-Gutman, Sonia.
  Teen pregnancy.
  Bibliography: p.
  Summary: Discusses the social, physical, and economic
problems of teenage pregnancy and parenthood and describes
various methods of birth control.
  1. Pregnancy, Adolescent—United States—Juvenile
literature. 2. Adolescent mothers—United States—
Juvenile literature. [1. Pregnancy. 2. Birth control.
3. Adolescent parents. 4. Unmarried mothers] I. Title.
HQ759.4.B68   1987   363.9'6'088055   87-2907
ISBN 0-8225-0039-6 (lib. bdg.)

Manufactured in the United States of America

1 2 3 4 5 6 7 8 9 10 97 96 95 94 93 92 91 90 89 88 87

Contents

Introduction

Each year more than a million American teenagers become pregnant. This means that about three thousand teenagers become pregnant every day. Four out of five of these girls are unmarried. Teenage pregnancy has become so common over the last fifteen years that the United States now has the highest adolescent pregnancy rate in the Western world.

About 450,000 American teens get abortions every year. More than 500,000 choose to have and to keep their babies. Most of them are single mothers. The rest, fewer than 100,000, put their babies up for adoption.

There are many reasons why unplanned pregnancy occurs. Carelessness is one of them. Some teenagers want to believe that they are carried away impulsively into sex, without any premeditation. They might believe that planning to have intercourse is somehow wrong. Many girls think pregnancy cannot happen to them, only to other people. Also, study after study indicates teenagers do not know enough about how to prevent pregnancy. A hundred other reasons exist as well.

If you are considering becoming sexually active, if you are already active, or if you just want to know about birth control and about what life is like for pregnant teens, you will find the information you need in this book. You will find out how different methods of birth control work, how you use them, and where you can go to get birth control products. You will also find out that saying no to sex is OK.

If you are now pregnant, or think you may be pregnant, you still need the information available in this book. What are your options? What is it like to be a teenage parent?

This book teaches you to know yourself and be prepared. It talks about sexuality and shows how you can take control of your life. It tells how to prevent pregnancy, and what your choices are if you become pregnant. It gives you the straight facts about pregnancy and teenage parenthood.

Chapter One
Values

American adolescents are far more sexually active today than any previous generation of teenagers. Sexual intercourse among unmarried teenage women increased by two-thirds during the 1970s. Experts estimate that more than 40 percent of all teens in the United States are now sexually active. Sexual intercourse is considered by many to be a "rite of passage" through adolescence.

There is more to sex than just "doing it." Sexual intercourse is a human activity that involves your body, your mind, and your emotions. It is something you should think about long before you decide to do it—or not do it.

This book supplies you with a good deal of information about sex and contraception. It cannot provide you with the values that tell you how to use this information in your life. You will have to develop these values yourself.

What are values? They are preferred standards of action or preferred goals. You learn values from your family, your school, your church, and other parts of society through words and actions. Your family, your school, and your church all have values of their own. You may agree or disagree with those values, but by now you have internalized them. That means that you know how your family, your church, and your school will expect you to react to any given situation. You may agree or disagree with your parents or your church, but you *know* what behaviors are acceptable to them.

Each set of values rests on people's basic beliefs about the sources of truth or authority. Because people disagree as to these sources, they use different standards for determining the relative worth of things.

Developing your own values is part of growing up. Your code of sexual behavior will become a part of your value system, and your sexual behavior will reflect your total philosophy of life.

Developing Your Own Value System

You are probably on the way to developing a code of moral behavior of your own, but you may never have thought about it systematically. First you need to ask yourself, "What kinds of behavior do I value? What tells me how to act?"

One way to discover what values you have learned is to find out the reasons for the rules you have been told to follow. For example, if you value saving money and working hard, you probably say it is because you believe that this behavior will make you rich. It is also because you think that being rich is a worthy goal in life, that being rich will make you happy, and that being happy is a good goal to aim at. Not everyone has the same goals, or the same values, because not everyone has the same beliefs. Not everyone believes that being rich is good for people, or even that personal happiness is necessary.

Your values about sexuality are complex because they combine spiritual and emotional values with physical and practical concerns. For example, do you think it is right or wrong to have sexual intercourse with someone before you are married? Why do you think so? What tells you it is right or wrong? If you think it is wrong, do you think you will have sex before you are married anyway? What other value or belief would cause you to override your first answer?

Now that you have an idea how to look for the beliefs that tell you how to act, examine these beliefs. Try them out and see if they fit you. No one is born with a value system. Everyone learns a moral code from others, and puts the pieces he or she gets from parents, church, friends, even television, together a little differently. Deciding on your own value system is hard. There are many voices today. Do you behave as your church tells you to, or as your friends expect you to? Until recently there was a consensus in society about what was right and what was wrong. That is no longer true. Rules are no longer universally accepted by all.

To understand what your values are, you have to know what is important to you. To some teenagers, material possessions are very important. Most work very hard to acquire these. Some, a very few, steal to acquire them. Wanting things is not bad in itself, but how one goes about acquiring them can be very bad.

To some teenagers, social activities are very important. Dates and parties are fun, but if you neglect your studies because you socialize all the time, you are giving more value to friends and fun than to your goals for the future. Are you sure you know whether you value fun *now* over enough money later? If you try so hard to have fun and be popular that you frequently regret the way you acted at the party the night before, are you in touch with your values?

Maybe you are a jock and spend lots of time on sports. Some athletes are willing to give up hours that might be spent on homework or on a part-time job, because they are looking for a chance at professional sports or a chance to be a high school hero. Some even give up a social life because they work so hard on athletics. Be sure you know what you give up by spending so much time in practice and competition. Be sure you know what you *might* get and what you *really* get from sports. Know what is important to you so you can make informed decisions about your future.

Many business enterprises define what they want and where they are going by setting goals and then listing ways to achieve those goals. This process gives them a picture of what they intend to accomplish. Successful people sometimes use the same method to plan their actions.

Keeping your values in mind when you make decisions is not hard. You just learn to think your way through situations that might affect your future. If you know the possible consequences of your actions, you will feel you have control over your own life. It is frustrating to feel controlled by events or by others. Choosing your own direction in life, on the other hand, is one of the rewards of maturity.

Whether you realize it or not, decisions you make in your teens can affect your whole life. You are likely to decide now about your future training and education and how to cope with social issues, friendship, and love. Pressure from peers makes these decisions difficult. It often seems easier to do what everyone else is doing than to think what *you* want to do and how you can accomplish it. That is all the more reason for you to figure out what is right for you.

Finding the right answer means getting to know who you are or what sort of a person you would like to be. What kind of life do you want? What are you looking for in the future? The more certain you are about your goals, the clearer your choice of actions appears because you can see how your decisions will affect your long-term goals.

You have probably heard the term "informed decision." It means a decision based on facts and thought and a feeling of "rightness," of being at home with yourself. Gathering factual information and knowing yourself are central to the process.

Making Decisions about Sexuality

Once you have thought about your values and have confidence in your ability to make decisions, you will be free to say no to sex until you are ready for it. When you arrive at your decision about whether to have a sexual relationship, and with whom, it will be through your own values.

To keep your sexual behavior under *your* control and in line with your values, you must think carefully in advance of any romantic situation. Make each decision a well-informed one. If you think through in advance what you want, your decision may be better for you than one you make in the excitement of a romantic moment. Sexual intercourse is not just a game. Like it or not, it has an emotional value for most people. And if it results in pregnancy or disease, or even feelings of guilt, it can affect your whole life.

Most teens past puberty have given some thought to their sexuality. The important thing is that you know yourself and your values. You must give serious consideration to them. Know what behavior you expect from yourself, and think about what you will feel like if your behavior doesn't measure up to your standards.

If you think carefully before you actually become involved, you may come to the conclusion sex is something you are not ready for. The choice about sex is yours—not your parents' or your friends', your boyfriend's or your girlfriend's, but yours. If you want to resist sexual involvement, you might not know what to say or do when confronted with pressures to go further than you want. Thinking about it ahead of time will give you the confidence to act the way *you* want.

Poor reasons to have sex are:
• **To make you more popular.** Do you want to be popular because you will have sex, or because people like you? Sex is a small part of most people's lives. "Friendship" based only on sex may not be very strong friendship.
• **To defy your parents.** In a way, having sex because your parents tell you not to is just like getting in the cookie jar when your mother told you not to. It doesn't prove that you are mature or independent. It just means that you are still letting your parents determine what you do.

· **To be one of the crowd.** "Everybody else does" doesn't mean *you* have to. And just because everybody else *says* they do doesn't mean that they really *do*. People exaggerate about sex because they think it makes them sound more mature.

· **To prove your "manhood" or "womanhood."** Almost anybody can have sex. It takes a lot more than intercourse to make a real man or a real woman and to prove that you are mature.

· **To avoid hurting someone's feelings.** No matter what he or she says, you probably won't hurt your friend's feelings if you refuse to have sex. But you might hurt your self-respect, and your future, if you do.

· **To be held and cuddled.** You can be held and cuddled without sex. The feeling of closeness you have during intercourse will not last very long, but the consequences of intercourse might.

· **To defend against loneliness.** Having sex might make you feel less lonely for a little while, but most people say that they feel even lonelier afterwards. Friendships will help banish loneliness, but a mere sexual relationship will probably make it seem worse.

Good reasons for having sex are: as an intense expression of love and desire, to share mutual pleasure when you are ready for it, and for reproduction (if you are in a good position to care for a baby). You will find that sexual intercourse means more to you and is more enjoyable if it is part of a mutually secure and satisfying relationship.

When you have to decide whether to have sex, make your decision as you would make any major decision in your life. Listen to your needs and your own values.

Remember that some teenagers of both sexes have decided for sexual intercourse and some have decided against it at this stage of their development. It is unrealistic to expect everyone to abstain from sex, and it is unrealistic to expect everyone to be ready for sex at the same age. A decision about sexual intercourse does not put you in a "good" or "bad" category. Do your best to come to the decision which you can live with, and act responsibly.

If you do decide to have intercourse, you have a second decision to make which can also affect the rest of your life. Do you want to become pregnant—do you want your girlfriend to become pregnant—or not? The next chapters give you the information you need to make this decision. They tell you how to keep from becoming pregnant, what to expect if you become pregnant, and what you can do if your pregnancy is unwanted.

Chapter Two
Money

Whether you are a man or a woman, the first question you have to ask yourself when you think about having sex is, "Can I afford to have a baby?" To be able to answer this question, you need to know a few hard economic facts.

Did you ever think of putting a price tag on yourself? Not on the things you own, like your stereo or your bicycle, but on yourself? You may not have thought about yourself that way, but you do have an economic value completely apart from the things you may own. In terms of money, you could say that you are worth just as much as you can earn. Of course, no economic price tag can measure your real value to your friends and family in things like friendship, a good sense of humor, love, and affection. But your own economic value is one of the things you need to think about when you think about teenage pregnancy.

You may have a part-time job and earn enough money to pay for most of your clothes or for most of the things you want to buy. But if you subtract the amount it costs your parents to raise you from infancy—for everything from food and medical care to the furniture you use and the space that you sleep in—you will find that you have cost your parents more than you can earn right now.

Two hundred years ago, you would have been a definite economic asset to your family. Back then, families worked together to support each other. On a farm you might have started feeding the chickens or hoeing plants when you were four. If your parents had a shop, they would have depended on your help. In those days children and teenagers could earn more for their family than they cost to feed and house.

You would have been a sort of social security system for your parents: they would have fed and housed you when you were young, and to repay them you would have fed and housed them when they were too old to work. For these reasons it was important for a family to have a lot of children.

But all that has changed. Now most people work in factories and offices away from the home. One parent might stay home and take care of the kids and house, but more and more, it takes two paychecks to support a family. In many instances both mother and father have to work outside the home. Now there are extra costs like rent or property taxes, and families cannot grow most of their food so they have to buy it.

What all this means is that the value has swung the other way. Children and teenagers have become an expense to their parents. Parents still love their children and still have them and raise them. But the family has changed a lot. As recently as twenty-five years ago, families of nine or ten children were common on the farm. How many people do you know now who come from families that large? People have fewer children now because children cost more and contribute less labor.

What does this mean to you? It means that if you become a parent you are facing a very expensive future. It costs over $200,000 to raise a child until he or she is old enough to leave home. Day care costs a lot as well. You may not be able to find a job that pays you more than you spend to have your baby taken care of. Even when your child is in school, you will have to worry about summer vacations and year-round expenses for food, clothes, and toys.

But the amount you pay to raise a child is only half of the cost of getting pregnant when you are still a teenager yourself. You may not have thought about the other half of the cost.

The complex world of today demands better educated workers than ever before. This means you had better have at least a high school diploma before entering the job market, or you could face a lifetime of minimum-wage jobs. The more education or training you can get, the better your chances for a really good job.

If you have a child while you are still in high school, you will find it much more difficult to stay in class. Finding the money for a trade school or college will also be more difficult. You may end up depending on your parents for support—assuming they are willing or able to help—at a time when friends your age are heading off to college or getting their own apartments. You may find it hard to become independent, and harder still to earn enough to live a life you can really enjoy. You may become socially isolated from your peers. You will have to become an adult while you are still a teenager, with all of an adult's worries and problems.

The cost of getting a newborn baby through his or her first year will be different for different people and in different states, cities, and hospitals. However, the lowest costs—if the birth and pregnancy are not complicated, if you use cloth diapers, if you buy the minimum in clothing, toys and equipment for the baby, if you breast-feed, and if you don't use day care—add up to about $4,000. The high end of the range—if you have to have a cesarean section, or if you decide to feed the baby formula, if you need to use day care, and so on—can easily top $10,000.

Contrast this with the cost of different kinds of birth control. Saying no costs $0. The cost of using condoms for one year is approximately $38. The cost of using birth control pills for one year is approximately $144. Many clinics dispense them at no charge.

Do you know how much a good used car costs?

Would you rather have a car or a baby at this stage of your life? Which would open up more possibilities for you?

Chapter Three
Your Health and Your Baby's Health

Pregnant teenagers and unwed mothers were once almost invisible, and they were certainly not discussed in "polite society." Thirty, even twenty years ago, unwed mothers were quickly married off in what used to be called a "shotgun wedding"—this implied that the bride's father was standing by with a shotgun to make sure the groom didn't change his mind. If a marriage was "impractical," the woman would discreetly disappear during "confinement" and then give up her baby for adoption. An unwed mother faced secrecy and a lack of options.

Now the shotgun marriage is a relic of the past. Most teens today deal with marriage with more realism than they do with pregnancy. Most pregnant teens don't marry the father of their baby. "Why compound my mistake?" said one. She felt it was a mistake to get pregnant, and she did not want to add to the mistake with an unrealistic marriage. She felt she was too young for motherhood and for marriage. The statistics on teenage divorces confirm the wisdom of her choice. Eighty percent of teen marriages will not last five years.

Today, because of better nutrition and other health factors, women menstruate earlier than they did a few years ago. In 1850, menstruation often did not begin until age sixteen and a half. Today the average age is twelve and a half. Now there are more years when a woman can become pregnant. Particularly alarming is the fact that since 1960, adolescent mothers have been getting younger. This is partly due to biology, and partly to changing sexual customs.

The decision to become a mother may well be the most important one you can make, because motherhood has the greatest impact on a woman's life. This is especially true for teenage mothers who keep their babies. Very few return to school after becoming pregnant and even fewer after giving birth. You may have friends who are pregnant and have dropped out of school. In some communities women stay in school, but they find it very difficult to continue studying, especially after they give birth. The work load is just too big.

Most teenage mothers must fall back on welfare or some kind of government benefits. It can be tough to get benefits, and even if the government will provide financial help, it will not pay much.

Teenage pregnancy has become a critical link in the "cycle of poverty." This refers to the fact that now there are young girls with babies whose mothers had babies in their teens and whose grandmothers also had babies in their teens. Sometimes four generations live in one house or apartment. Many of these mothers are high school dropouts with little education and little chance to earn an adequate living now or in the future.

If the father acknowledges his responsibility and offers his help, the mother may still not be much better off. Teenage fathers usually have lower incomes and less education than men who wait until they are at least twenty to have children. Teen fathers often drop out of school when their girlfriends get pregnant. That only compounds the problem, because lack of a high school degree limits their earning ability for the present and the future.

The project director of the Bank Street College Study of Teenage Parents believes "A lot of teenage fathers want to love their babies and do the right thing for them, but they don't see how to do what is right." Many doubt their abilities as providers. Most are simply not able to earn enough to provide for themselves and their families and to continue their education or training. Without education, their prospects for better jobs at better pay are very slim.

This sad picture does not begin to describe the loneliness, discontent, and sense of isolation a teenage mother often experiences. Teenage mothers attempt suicide seven times more often than their contemporaries. Apparently, many see no other way out of their situation. They don't realize that there are other options.

One of the most important aspects of pregnancy for the teen mother as well as for her baby is *prenatal* (before birth) care. Health problems during pregnancy occur more often for girls under fifteen than for women aged twenty to twenty-four. Problems can be minimized with early and regular prenatal care, but many teenagers don't seek prenatal care because they are afraid to tell their parents they are pregnant. Many lack information about available clinics or services for teenagers, or lack transportation.

Even under the best conditions and with the best care, pregnancy is not good for the health of teenagers or their babies. There are serious health risks to young teens who bear children. Their bodies are still growing and developing. The strain of pregnancy often leads to increased high blood pressure. *Toxemia* (a form of blood poisoning) and problems during labor and delivery are also common when the pelvis is not completely grown. Due to these hazards, the death rate is sixty percent higher among pregnant teenagers under the age of fifteen than among older girls and women.

Good nutrition is another important part of a healthy pregnancy that results in a healthy mother and well baby. It is hard for pregnant adults to stick to the proper diet during pregnancy, and it can be harder for teens to pass up the food all of their friends still eat. Candy bars, potato chips, and pop are not good for the health of a fetus or a pregnant mother. Because a teenage body is still growing and needs good nutrition for itself, a pregnant teenager who doesn't eat right may force her body to fight with her baby for vitamins, proteins, and carbohydrates each needs. *Everything* a pregnant mother eats, drinks, breathes, or takes into her body in any form affects her baby. Smoking is bad for the baby. Drinking alcohol, including wine and beer, is bad for the baby. Any other drugs and medicines— even aspirin—which have not been prescribed by a physician are dangerous to the developing baby and the pregnant mother.

Babies born to teenagers are twice as likely to die before their first birthday as are babies born to women in their twenties. Teenagers' babies also run a higher risk of being premature. Premature babies suffer from low birth weight and frequent respiratory problems. These babies are also more likely to have physical and/or mental handicaps. Low birth weight is often a major cause of infant mortality, birth injuries, mental retardation, and neurological defects. The younger the teenage mother, the higher the likelihood of infant death in the first year. The baby's health may therefore require extra care and extra expenses.

Day-to-day care of a baby is hard work. Most teenagers have not had time to learn all they need to know about being a parent. Because of this, babies of teenage mothers face increased risks of illness, injury, or death. Babies of teenagers are more likely to suffer from accidents, undiagnosed illnesses, inadequate nutrition, neglect or abuse, and environmental hazards.

Teenagers *can* have safe pregnancies and raise well babies. There are clinics and organizations that will help with information and support. This chapter was simply an attempt to warn you of the risks you and your baby would face. If you want to avoid those risks, you can learn to prevent an unwanted pregnancy.

Chapter Four
Conception and Contraception

The nature of adolescence—a period when the young person is separating from the family and seeking independence—is changing. The moral code dealing with sex has become less restrictive. Sexual intercourse is a much bigger factor in the lives of American teens today than it was a few years ago. Young people are more open about sex. They grow up surrounded by sex in movies and television shows, in novels that leave little to the imagination, and in advertisements. Sex, blatant or subtle, is the basis of many television commercials. And because of better health and nutrition, young people mature more quickly now than they did one hundred years ago.

One of the outcomes of these divergent forces—better health, faster physical maturation, and less restrictive sex—has been an increase in teenage pregnancies. One

American teenage girl in ten becomes pregnant, and most of those pregnancies are unintended and therefore unnecessary.

Most teens have sex for about twelve months before they start using contraceptives. Experts estimate that only one in three sexually active teens *regularly* uses birth control. Also, a number of studies indicate that teenagers know very little about birth control.

Here are some birth control *facts* that may interest you:

Fact: Eighty percent of sexually active teenage girls who don't use birth control get pregnant *the very first month of active sex.*

Fact: A woman can get pregnant even if she has sex infrequently. As the saying goes, "It only takes once."

Fact: A woman can get pregnant using the withdrawal method, because even a very small drop of semen can produce a baby—and some semen often oozes out even before the man climaxes or "comes."

Here are a few *myths* about birth control:

Myth: *Women cannot get pregnant the first time.* Remember, "It only takes once."

Myth: *If the woman douches afterward, she won't get pregnant.* Sperm move so quickly that some will have swum beyond the reach of any douche within ninety seconds of intercourse.

Myth: *Women can't get pregnant if they have sex standing up.* In reality, sperm are very active little cells. They can swim uphill as easily as salmon swim upstream.

Myth: *Men don't have responsibility for contraception.* Birth control is the responsibility of *both* partners.

Myth: *You have to be fifteen years old to buy birth control paraphernalia.* Not so. You can buy it at any age.

Myth: *A girl under fifteen is too young to get pregnant.* Chronological age has nothing to do with it, it is physical maturity that counts. Many girls get pregnant at age twelve, or even younger. You can even get pregnant before you have had your first period.

Myth: *If the woman urinates right after intercourse, she can't get pregnant.* Since urine comes out a different passageway from the one the sperm are swimming up, urinating won't wash them away.

Contraception is the name given to techniques and devices which prevent pregnancy. Only about a third of the sexually active American girls between the ages of fifteen and nineteen use contraceptives. The average teen waits twelve months after the first sexual involvement before seeking contraception information. If you are thinking about becoming sexually active or are already sexually active, you need this information.

You are gambling with your future if you have sexual intercourse without giving it some thought and without being prepared. Thinking ahead and planning aren't the same as being calculating. They show you are wise, considerate, realistic, and mature. Even if you are not in love with anyone yet, be *realistic* and be *prepared*.

An unwanted pregnancy forces you to choose between parenthood, adoption, or abortion. This is an extremely difficult choice to make. Considering what kind of contraception is best suited for you is quite simple by comparison.

For each person, one birth control method is best. What is important is how you and your partner feel about it and whether or not you use the method correctly and consistently. Whichever method you choose, it is up to you to make that method work. If you choose to say no, it is up to you to make it work every time.

Any honest and responsible relationship that includes sex also includes contraception. The best way to go about getting information is for both of you to go to a physician or a clinic for medically-supervised help. Prevention of pregnancy is the responsibility of both of you. There are many free clinics serving teenagers. If one of you is too embarrassed, too shy, or too insecure to get contraceptive advice, you are not ready for sexual intercourse with each other. If you are responsible enough to have a sexual relationship, you are responsible enough to consider the risks involved in sex. It is easy to get pregnant, so you should use effective birth control *every time*.

Conception

In order for you to understand how the different kinds of birth control work, you first must understand how conception occurs. Conception happens when a *sperm* cell from a man's body enters an *ovum* (mature egg cell) inside a woman's body. Conditions must be right for the sperm to meet the ovum. However, it is difficult for you to know when conditions are right, so conception could happen any time you have sex—if you don't take precautions.

Sperm cells look like tiny tadpoles and propel themselves by their long tails. Sperm is produced in the *testicles*

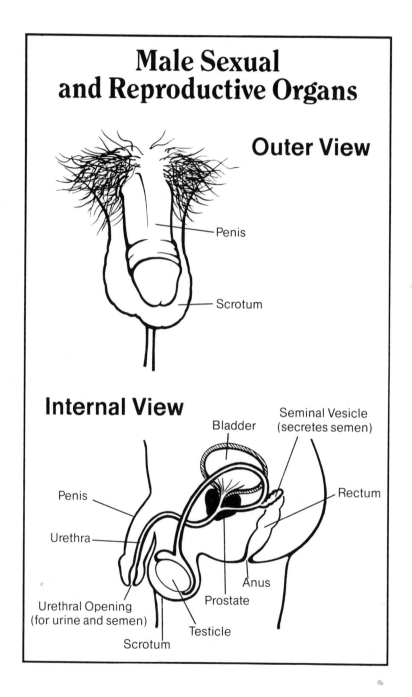

Male Sexual and Reproductive Organs

Outer View

Penis

Scrotum

Internal View

Bladder

Seminal Vesicle
(secretes semen)

Penis

Rectum

Urethra

Urethral Opening
(for urine and semen)

Prostate

Anus

Scrotum

Testicle

(balls). They are in the wrinkled sac called the *scrotum*. A gland called the *prostate* makes a fluid called *seminal fluid*. When a man *ejaculates* or has an orgasm, the sperm cells are released from the penis in the seminal fluid. The mixture of fluid and sperm is called *semen*.

Semen travels through the penis in a narrow tube, the *urethra*. This tube also carries urine from the bladder through the penis, but it cannot carry both urine and semen at the same time. When a man is sexually aroused, the flow of urine to the urethra is shut off so that only semen can get through.

A woman's body produces egg cells or ova in two organs called *ovaries*. The ovaries are on either side of the *uterus* or womb, which is where a baby grows until it is ready to be born. A pair of tubes called *Fallopian tubes* extend from the uterus to just above the ovaries.

About every twenty-eight days an ovum ripens. This means that it is ready to accept a sperm cell or be fertilized. A ripe ovum is a little smaller than the period at the end of this sentence. The ripe egg cell bursts out of the ovaries and begins to travel through one of the Fallopian tubes toward the uterus. The egg's trip through the Fallopian tube is called *ovulation*.

While the egg is still in the ovary, the uterus begins to change. The layers of cells in its lining begin to grow and thicken to provide a place for a fertilized egg. If the egg is not fertilized, then the thickened lining breaks down and the woman's body gets rid of it as *menstrual flow*. The process of shedding this unused lining is called *menstruation* and it takes about four or five days. Then the cycle begins again—if the egg was not fertilized.

When you have intercourse, the man's erect penis enters

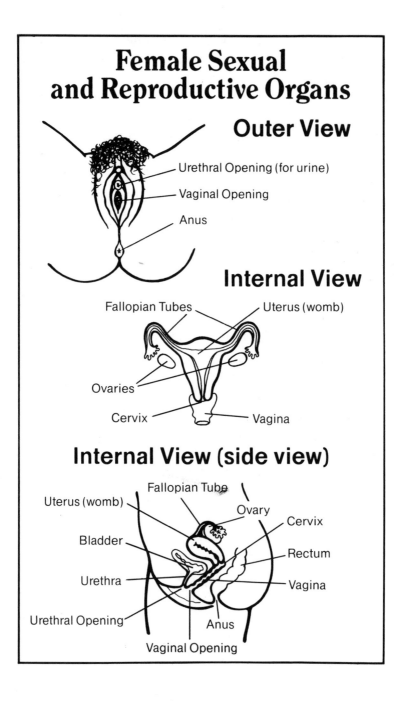

Female Sexual and Reproductive Organs

Outer View

- Urethral Opening (for urine)
- Vaginal Opening
- Anus

Internal View

- Fallopian Tubes
- Uterus (womb)
- Ovaries
- Cervix
- Vagina

Internal View (side view)

- Uterus (womb)
- Fallopian Tube
- Ovary
- Cervix
- Bladder
- Rectum
- Urethra
- Vagina
- Urethral Opening
- Anus
- Vaginal Opening

the vagina. Although the penis is usually limp and soft, when a man is sexually excited it fills with blood and becomes firm so that it can enter the *vagina*. The vagina leads to the woman's uterus. When the man reaches climax, semen is ejaculated from the penis. If any sperm land inside the vagina or even near enough to the vagina to reach it before they die, they can make the journey and fertilize a waiting egg.

After the sperm cells enter the vagina, they swim into the uterus, and then up into the Fallopian tubes. If a sperm meets an ovum while it is still in the Fallopian tube, conception takes place. The ovum takes several days to travel to the uterus, and conception is possible any time during ovulation. Sperm can live in the uterus up to five days, so intercourse even five days before ovulation can leave sperm around to fertilize the egg. If the egg is fertilized, it will travel on and attach itself inside the uterus. The fertilized egg is called an *embryo* until the end of the eighth week. Later it is called a *fetus,* later still a baby.

Methods of Contraception

The basic idea of contraception is to keep the egg and the sperm from getting together. If you decide to have intercourse, you can choose from two categories of birth control. One category requires a medical exam and the other does not. The first includes the pill, IUD, and the diaphragm, all contraceptive devices used by women. The second category includes devices which do not require a medical examination: condoms (used by males), creams, suppositories, the sponge, the rhythm method or fertility awareness, and the withdrawal method.

Saying No to Intercourse

The most certain method of birth control is saying no to sexual intercourse. This does not mean you cannot be sexual at all. You can hug and kiss and touch each other without intercourse. You can even bring each other to orgasm without sexual intercourse. If you want to try out your sexual feelings, or enjoy closeness with someone, but are not ready for the risks and commitment of intercourse, this may be the best option for you. This is the only type of contraception that is 100% effective.

Condom (Rubber, Skin, Sheath)

The condom is a thin tube, closed at one end. It is placed over the erect penis just before intercourse. All condoms made in the United States have to meet government standards for reliability. One size fits everybody (really).

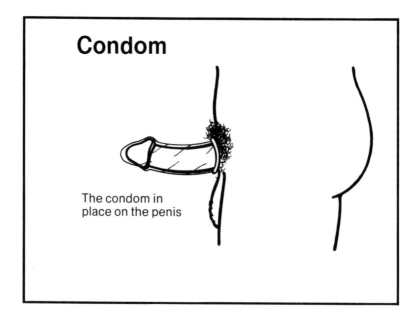

Condom

The condom in place on the penis

You can purchase condoms at your local drugstore or your local family planning center.

When you place the condom on the penis, leave at least one-half inch of slack at the end of the condom to collect semen. You can also purchase condoms with a reservoir tip (a built-in space at the tip of the condom) which will collect the semen. Hold the condom closed when the penis is withdrawn from the vagina so as not to spill *any* semen. Make sure the condom does not slip off as the penis is withdrawn from the vagina.

When you purchase condoms, you have a choice of colors: no color, or black, red, blue, green, or orange. Condoms can be purchased one at a time, in packs of three or in boxes of a dozen. You can also obtain condoms that are prelubricated. Do not use vaseline or anything else with oil in it as a lubricant because oil weakens rubber. K-Y jelly or saliva are good lubricants.

Of 100 couples relying on condoms, about 10 pregnancies may occur in the first year of use. If the woman uses a vaginal foam at the same time the man uses a condom, the protection is greater. Using a condom can protect partners from sharing veneral diseases, such as herpes or gonorrhea, and it is hoped that condoms provide protection from AIDS as well. Condoms can be carried in a wallet, pocket, or purse. Keep them in their sealed wraps and away from extreme heat or cold.

Contraceptive Foams, Creams, Jellies, and Suppositories

Contraceptive foams, creams, jellies, and suppositories can usually be found in drug stores on the display shelves next to the sprays and douches for "feminine hygiene." You

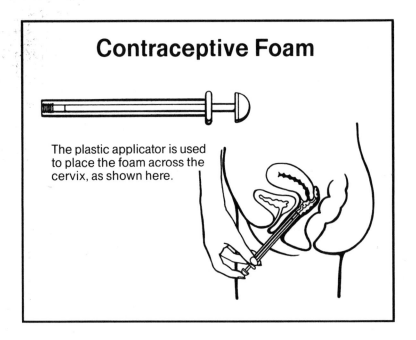

Contraceptive Foam

The plastic applicator is used to place the foam across the cervix, as shown here.

can also obtain them at family planning centers. In the store, look for those boxes that are clearly marked "contraceptive" or "spermicidal" (sperm-killing).

The foam is not scented, and it is absorbed much like hand lotion. It must be placed in the vagina near the *cervix* (the opening of the uterus) before intercourse. It does not drip out of the vagina.

Foam contains a spermicidal chemical that destroys the coating of the sperm head. It is not necessary to wash foam out after each intercourse. If you want to douche after sex, give the foam eight hours to finish its job.

The first time you buy foam you will need a kit that has an applicator in it. After the initial purchase, you can just buy refills. It is usually a good idea to keep at least one refill on hand, since it is hard to tell when the supply is running low.

Foam has to be inserted into the vagina before the penis enters. Apply it no more than twenty minutes before intercourse. If it turns out to be more like an hour before intercourse, add another application. If you have sex again later on, repeat the application again.

Insert the applicator in the vagina like you insert a tampon. Slide it in as far as it will go, until it bumps against the cervix. Then press the plunger slowly as far as it will go. Put the applicator and the container where you can reach them later, just in case.

Every foam kit includes a plastic case that holds the container and applicator. The kit takes up about as much room as a couple of tampons, which makes it easy to carry.

Contraceptive creams and jellies are substances a woman inserts into her vagina just before sexual intercourse. They block off the entrance to the uterus and kill the sperms. They come in tubes. Suppositories are pellets that are inserted by hand into the vagina. The movements of intercourse help melt the pellets and mix them with your body fluids. Creams, jellies, and suppositories are not as reliable as medical methods, but they are easy to purchase and to use. Of 100 women using chemical vaginal contraceptives, about 18 may become pregnant in the first year of use. If you use both foam and condoms, you increase your protection.

Sponge

The sponge looks like a small doughnut with a hollow or dimple in its center instead of a hole. This hollow area fits over the cervix. The sponge measures about one and

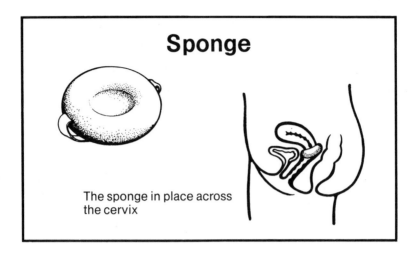

Sponge

The sponge in place across
the cervix

three-quarters of an inch in diameter. It is made out of a
sponge-like material filled with the same spermicide used
in foams, jellies, and creams.

The sponge has a loop of polyester tape across the
bottom for ease of removal. The sponge feels a little like a
foam rubber pillow. While in place, it is meant to protect
against pregnancy for twenty-four hours. It is available
without prescription at a drugstore or at your family
planning clinic. It is important to know the proper way to
position it inside the body, so you may want to get
instruction and practice in this.

Once the sponge is in place you can have repeated
sexual intercourse within a twenty-four-hour period without
further precautions. You must leave the sponge in place
for at least six hours after the last time you have sex. If it is
used *perfectly* every time, between nine and eleven percent
of users will become pregnant. In actuality, because of
factors such as improper placement and removal too soon

after intercourse, it is less effective than this. Using the sponge with another contraceptive method, like the condom, will increase your protection.

The Withdrawal Method

The withdrawal method is the removal of the penis from the vagina just before a man reaches his climax or "comes." This is supposed to keep sperm cells out of the vagina. It is unreliable for most young people because it requires a great deal of control by the man. Even with excellent control it is risky, because some sperm are released from the penis involuntarily before the climax. Pregnancy can occur even if semen is deposited on a woman's external sex organs.

This method of contraception is included here for information only. It is *not* recommended for teens. Its effectiveness is *very* uncertain.

Periodic Abstinence, The Rhythm Method, or Natural Family Planning

Periodic abstinence requires a couple to avoid sex during the time of a woman's fertile period. These are the days just before, during, and right after an egg is released. To determine when this is likely to happen each month, the woman takes her temperature and/or examines her vaginal mucus every day. She may also keep track of her cycle on a calendar. A woman's body temperature usually drops twenty-four to thirty-six hours before the egg is released, and then rises after ovulation.

This method requires a great deal of regularity, discipline, and record-keeping. It is hard for teens to adjust to. It takes careful observation and a sensitive thermometer, because the temperature drop is only two to three-tenths of a degree and the rise only seven to eight-tenths of a degree. This method will not work if a woman's period is irregular. Illness or physical or emotional stress can change the timing of a woman's fertile period. It is a *very* uncertain method of contraception and *not* recommended for teenagers.

Birth Control Pills (The Pill)

A woman can prevent an unwanted pregnancy by using birth control pills, most often referred to as "the pill."

The use of the pill requires a doctor's or clinician's prescription. You must follow instructions carefully. Should you forget to take a pill for two or more days in a row, don't try to make up for it by taking several pills at once. A prescription for birth control pills can be filled at a drugstore, pharmacy, or family planning center.

There are many types of pills made up of different combinations and amounts of two hormones, *estrogen* and *progestin*. These stop the woman's ovaries from releasing an egg each month, so that there is never an egg to meet the sperm. The pill must be taken on a regular, daily schedule. You need to be on the pill for at least ten days before it is effective. You should never borrow pills from anyone else. Taking the pill only before or after having sex will not prevent pregnancy.

Not all teenagers should use the pill. If you have not yet started having regular periods you probably should not be on it. Pills may be dangerous if you are a smoker. Some teens have problems such as weight gain, nausea, or headaches when they take the pill. For most people these are temporary setbacks. Serious complications are rare but may occur in some people. These are blood-clotting disorders with symptoms such as severe headaches, leg pain, chest pains, abdominal pain, or blurred vision. If you have any of these problems while you are taking the pill, you should call a doctor or clinic right away. These side effects are the reason why the pill is only sold with a prescription from a doctor or clinic.

The pill also has positive side effects. According to the Alan Guttmacher Institute, there are fewer ovarian cysts among women who use the pill, fewer cases of PID (pelvic inflammatory disease), and fewer cases of anemia. In addition, the pill tends to reduce cramps or heavy menstrual flow.

Of 100 women on the pill, about 2 may become pregnant during the first year of use. Women who never forget to take the pill and who take it at the same time each day will have less chance of getting pregnant.

Diaphragm

The diaphragm is a flexible rubber cup that is inserted deep inside the vagina before intercourse. Diaphragms come in different sizes, and a doctor has to fit you with the proper size.

The diaphragm covers the cervix so sperm cannot enter the uterus. It is used in combination with sperm-killing jelly or cream, which is placed on the rim and dome of the diaphragm before inserting it into the vagina. This prevents fertilization in two ways: it poses a physical barrier to the sperm, and the jelly or cream kills the sperm. A diaphragm must be inserted before intercourse, but you can put it in as long as six hours before. If either partner can feel the diaphragm during intercourse or if it is uncomfortable, it

Diaphragm

The diaphragm is spread with contraceptive jelly or cream.

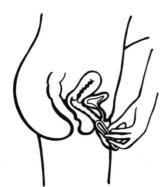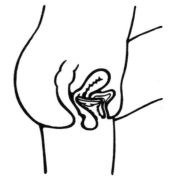

Then it is folded with the jelly or cream inside and inserted into the vagina so it covers the cervix.

either doesn't fit or was not properly placed. It should be checked by your doctor.

The diaphragm should be left in place for eight hours after intercourse. This gives the jelly or cream time to kill the sperm. Should you have intercourse again before the eight hours are up, be sure to add more jelly or cream. Do not take out the diaphragm to do this.

Eight hours after the last time you have had sex, you can take the diaphragm out, wash it, rinse it, and dry it carefully. Dust it with cornstarch and put it back into its container. You should check it for holes every so often by looking through it at a light.

Because the proportions of each individual are different, you cannot use anyone else's if you want to be safe from getting pregnant. If you gain or lose ten pounds, you will need to be refitted. After you are fitted for a diaphragm, you can purchase it at your local drugstore or at your local family planning clinic. Practice inserting it until you are sure that you know the right way to do this.

Of 100 women using diaphragms, about 19 may become pregnant during the first year of use. You can increase your protection by checking that it is properly in position every time you have intercourse.

IUD

IUD stands for *intrauterine device*. It is a small piece of flexible plastic or metal that is inserted into the uterus by a physician to prevent pregnancy. The doctor will teach you how to check your IUD periodically to make sure it is in place. IUDs come in different shapes and sizes. It is *not* considered to be a good birth control method for teenagers, because infections associated with the IUD can make it

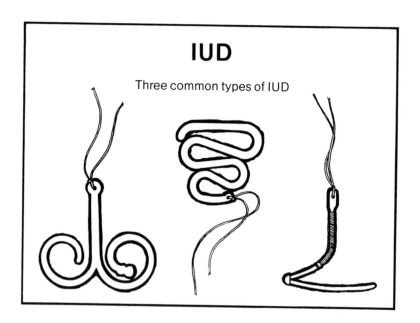

IUD

Three common types of IUD

more difficult for a woman to get pregnant later on.

The IUD has become very controversial in the last few years, and many clinics and doctors oppose its use. Nobody knows exactly how it works to stop pregnancy. Possibly it makes it more difficult for the egg and sperm to meet. It may stop a fertilized egg from attaching itself to the wall of the uterus so it can grow.

The IUD sometimes can cause extra cramps and bleeding during menstrual periods. This may stop after a couple of months. If it does not, you should see your clinician or doctor. Some IUD users have more serious problems such as infections. If you have abdominal pains, bleeding, chills and fever, or unpleasant discharge, you may have an infection and need to be seen by a doctor right away.

Of 100 women with IUDs, about 5 may become pregnant

during the first year of use. The longer you use the IUD, the less the likelihood of pregnancy. You can increase your protection by checking regularly to be sure it's in place, and by using foam or condoms for a week about midway between periods.

Abortion is not listed above because it is not a method of contraception. It does not prevent the sperm and egg from meeting. Abortion is a method of birth control by taking the fertilized egg, embryo, or fetus out of the woman's body.

Each method of birth control described in this chapter has a rate of failure. You can minimize the risk by using your chosen method correctly and consistently every time. Some methods guaranteed not to work any time are: hoping, petroleum jelly, douching, and mind-altering drugs.

Chapter Five
The Egg and I:
A Parenting Game

If you engage in sex, you should be mature enough and knowledgeable enough to take sensible precautions against unwanted pregnancy. Having a baby is one of the most important decisions a person can make. It is also irreversible. You have probably seen the ads that tell you, "It's like being grounded for eighteen years."

When you are involved with someone and there is a chance you might have intercourse, think about it before you go ahead with it. Be honest with yourself. Admit that you are a sensitive human being with normal sexual needs. Most teens fulfill their sexual needs without having intercourse. Must your fulfillment include intercourse? If you decide the answer is yes, be responsible to yourself and your partner. Talk it over with him or her. Consider the risks involved. Be prepared. Without birth control, it is easy to get pregnant. If you are having intercourse, use *effective* birth control *every time.*

Shared responsibility is important in a love relationship. So is communication. Let your partner know how you feel about him or her, about sex, about contraception, about your future. Is your partner listening? Does he or she really hear what you are saying?

Think about your relationship and about the chance of pregnancy before you have intercourse. If you have sex with your boyfriend does that automatically mean he loves you? Or just that he wants to have sex? If you get pregnant, will he marry you? If you get pregnant in the hope that a boyfriend will marry you, you are gambling with your life and your baby's: what are your chances that you and your baby will be left alone?

If you do get pregnant before you are ready, what will you do? If you decide to keep the baby, are you willing to be committed to its welfare for the next eighteen to twenty years? Who should be responsible for your baby? You, the baby's father, your parents, society at large?

Babies need and deserve to be wanted, loved, and supported. So do you. Allow yourself time to grow up before you become a mother or father.

How do you know if you are "parental material"? Ask yourself questions like these: What do I want out of life for myself? Am I ready to give up the freedom to do what I want to do, when I want to do it? Would I miss my free time and my privacy? Does my partner want a baby? Is our relationship really strong and happy? Do we understand each other's feelings about religion, work, family, child-raising, and future goals? Suppose one of us wants a child and the other does not: who decides what happens?

Some counseling clinics and schools try to help teenagers make the right choice at the right time about motherhood and fatherhood. They try to show them what parenthood is really like. One of the ways they do it is with "The Egg and I" game. This is how it is played.

A counselor can lead the game, or a group of teenagers can choose one of their own as a leader. The leader then asks the group to describe the difference between an egg and a baby. Commonly, the group decides that an egg is cheaper, quieter, neater—but both are fragile.

Then the leader gets eggs from the refrigerator and passes them around. The group is told that these eggs are now their "babies," to protect and care for. They will use the eggs to try to get a feeling for the responsibility and consistency of care needed to be a mother or a father.

The leader can put a blue dot or a pink dot on each egg to convey the idea of a "boy" or a "girl." The "babies" can be dressed up by the "parents" to give them more personality.

Now the group leader asks questions of individual teenagers in the group: What will you name your baby? Where will you keep it? What will you feed it? How will you pay for the doctor's bills? Individuals think the questions through and play at the role of parenthood.

Sometimes teens are sent home with the "baby" and are expected to take total responsibility for it for twenty-four hours a day—or sometimes an entire week. At all times the "mother" or "father" must be caring for it, or it must be "sleeping" safely in the constant care of a sitter. The parent must handle the "baby" gently, as if it were a real baby and could be hurt by rough treatment, by cold drafts, or by being ignored. Can the parent find a babysitter? Can he or she pay for the babysitter? After a few days of this kind of role-playing, a pretty clear picture emerges about the real demands of motherhood. And at the end of a week of "parenthood," very few "babies" are still unbroken.

Some counselors ask that teens keep a journal throughout the week of their activities and feelings about their new "responsibilities." They ask questions like, "What did you feel like when you got up for the 2:00 A.M. feeding and the 6:00 A.M. feeding?" "How would you feel if you had to do this every night?" "Was it hard to think about keeping the baby safe every minute of every day? Did you feel tied down?" "If you had to be a parent for real, would you still have the energy to do other things?"

This kind of intensive role-playing gives teens a pretty realistic idea of the changes a baby would bring to their lives—changes in daily routine, in the amount of shared (or not shared) responsibility with the father of the baby, and in the amount of energy and financial resources you would need.

The more realistically you play the game and the longer you play it, the more you can learn about your parenting readiness.

Chapter Six
Case Stories

What happens if you do find yourself pregnant? First, don't panic. Consider all of your options. These case stories will show you how some other teenagers have handled their sexuality and the problems that arise because of it. No single solution is the right one for everybody. There are choices. There are doctors, counselors, clinics, and parents to help you sort out your feelings and your options.

No matter how desperate your situation seems, there is help. Millions of teenagers have been in your position over the centuries. They have made decisions and survived. So will you.

Susie

Susie became pregnant at sixteen. When the thought first struck her that she might be pregnant, she tried to put it out of her mind. She pretended, even to herself, that she wasn't really worried, because it couldn't really be true. This wouldn't happen to *her*.

When she missed her second period, she went to the doctor for a pregnancy test. The result was positive.

When the doctor told her the test result, she said, "Susie, you need to make up your mind very soon about what you want to do." The doctor suggested she talk to her parents about her pregnancy. She explained that Susie could keep the baby, put the baby up for adoption, or have an abortion. If Susie thought she would want to have an abortion, then the decision needed to be made soon. The longer she waited the more complicated and dangerous an abortion would become.

Susie was facing a crisis and she needed to act. She dreaded talking to her parents. Sex was not openly discussed at home. Her mother had talked to her about menstruation when Susie was about ten years old. Sex had not been mentioned since then. Even so, Susie knew that her mother would be easier to talk to than her father. Although her mother was reluctant to talk about sexual matters, Susie knew that in the end she would be her ally.

For ten more days she agonized. Finally she told her mother, who told her father. Both were angry at Susie and very ashamed of her pregnancy. But at least she was no longer alone. It was not just *her* crisis, it was a family crisis now.

Abortion was not an option for Susie because of her religious beliefs. Susie and her parents agreed that abortion was impossible.

While they were looking at ways to deal with the "problem," they continued to argue and fight with each

other and with other family members. Rumors about
Susie's pregnancy circulated among her friends. Some of
Susie's friends dropped her. Others continued to treat her
the same as always. The boy who was the baby's father no
longer saw her. Tension escalated all around Susie, at
home and at school. Finally she dropped out of school.

Life at home was not pleasant either. Her parents
blamed Susie for what had happened, then each other,
then the state of the world. Finally, the bad feelings
subsided somewhat. Susie began to feel her mother's
support, and that gave her strength. She decided she
would have the baby and live with her parents, and see
how things went. Everyone agreed to this, and for a while
life went on almost normally.

The baby was born and everything went well. Susie
named him Jason. She came home from the hospital with
the baby to live with her family. Both of her parents were
supportive now. Occasionally Susie had free time because
her mother would baby-sit. Since her parents supported
her and the baby, Susie had no financial worries. But their
relationships had changed.

Susie was now a mother herself and had more responsibilities than before. She resented her mother's bossiness
and the way she told her what to do for Jason. After all, he
was *her* baby, to raise the way she wanted. Susie didn't
participate in normal teenage activities. She still had to
ask to borrow the car, and her father still gave her a curfew
if she went out. She was sort of suspended between two
worlds—the grownup world of parents and the teenage
world of school and social activities.

There began to be frequent fights at home. Susie felt
she was being treated like a child. She wanted and needed

more independence. Her room was cluttered, she couldn't sleep, she was tired all the time and felt very restricted. The baby also disrupted her parents' household. They were no longer used to a baby's cry, to diapers, and to early morning feeding noises.

Susie moved out and rented a small apartment with an older girl who worked. Her mother gave her a little money, just enough for two months' rent. Her parents let her take the furniture from her room and the baby furniture she had gotten. She bought pots and pans from a thrift shop and the Salvation Army.

Susie envied her roommate's independence. Some of Susie's friends from school visited her, but they no longer had much in common. Susie was tied down with Jason and could not go out with them. She had enough money for an occasional movie, but not for a baby-sitter *and* a movie.

Because she needed money, Susie applied for financial assistance from the state and county. She eventually received a little less than a hundred dollars a month. The social worker told her the government was rethinking financial assistance and there was no guarantee how long the money would continue. Susie's parents were relieved she now had some income, but embarrassed about having a daughter and grandchild on welfare.

After three or four months, Susie decided this was not her kind of life. She spent all of her time caring for Jason. She sat around and watched television, and if she did go out she had to take Jason with her. She had no social life. She considered giving up her baby for adoption and even visited an adoption agency. She talked with a county social worker.

In the end, she placed Jason in a welfare day-care center

and went back to a different high school. She wanted to learn enough to earn a living for herself and the baby. Meanwhile, she survived on welfare, food stamps, and an occasional check from her mother.

Karen and Tim

Karen and Tim dated for seven months in their senior year at high school. They were very much in love. When Karen became pregnant, they were stunned. Then they blamed each other for the pregnancy. It almost broke up the relationship. Finally they realized that they were *both* responsible for the pregnancy. When they faced that fact, the good feelings they had for each other resurfaced.

Karen and Tim decided to get married and keep the baby. When they told their parents, they heard everything from "Over my dead body!" to "Where did we go wrong?" They stood firm. In the end, their parents accepted the fact that Karen and Tim were going to get married.

They married right after graduation and rented a small apartment. Their baby, Melissa, was born three months later. Karen's and Tim's parents loved their grandchild and visited occasionally. Tim's parents bought a new crib for Melissa and gave Karen and Tim a rocking chair as a present. Beyond that, Karen, Tim, and the baby were financially on their own.

Karen explained their decision to get married: "Our parents, everyone said we were too young. But the baby was on the way, and we were very much in love, so we wanted to have the baby. It's very hard now. The biggest problem is money. Tim works too hard, and it seems he's gone all the time."

Karen's high school friends occasionally stopped by to

visit and see how they were managing. They saw how restricted her life was. She couldn't earn any money to help with expenses. She hadn't found a day-care center that was cheap enough to let her get a job, so she was stuck at home.

Both Karen and Tim had wanted to go on to college and had often talked about different career paths they might follow. Now Tim worked as a busboy in a local restaurant. Two or three nights a week he helped out in a nursing home. Karen and Tim would still like to go on to college in order to get a chance at better-paying jobs. Right now that is impossible. Tim's wages barely cover necessities such as rent and food.

In the meantime, Karen is quite frustrated. She would like to go out and earn some money. She is tired of being with the baby all day, seven days a week. "Our friends are coming less and less to visit," Karen said. "A lot of them have gone off to college somewhere. The others don't seem to want to bother with people who have a baby to take care of. And anyway, we seem to have much less in common than we used to."

Karen and Tim love each other, but they both wonder how long they can live without anyone or anything to ease the grinding pressure and boredom of their everyday life. They wonder what life will be like for them two or even five years from now.

Jane

Jane was in tenth grade and doing well. She was ambitious and hardworking and was doing very well in school. She had her sights set on studying communications in college. She wanted to become a television producer.

Then she started going out with Chuck. She had not dated much before. Chuck was different. They both liked to ski, they enjoyed the same movies. They had been seeing each other for four months when it happened.

One day after cross-country skiing they got carried away, and for the first time went beyond kissing and petting. It was not planned and they had never discussed their physical relationship, contraception, or how far they were prepared to go with each other. Jane and Chuck had not had much interest in or much education about sex until recently. They knew very little about contraception.

Jane got pregnant the first time they had intercourse. When the doctor confirmed the diagnosis, Jane was stunned. She called Chuck and told him right away. He had been expecting the call because he knew she had gone to the doctor for a pregnancy test. They decided to get some counseling at the neighborhood teenage health clinic.

The counselor at the clinic discussed their options with them and suggested they tell their parents. Jane was confused and upset. She knew that she had choices to make. She loved Chuck, but she wasn't ready for marriage or for motherhood.

Chuck was scared to become a parent, too. He talked to the counselor and listened to Jane and the counselor talking. However, he began to feel left out. The decision was Jane's, not his, and he did not think that if he disagreed with her it would make much difference.

Jane's parents supported Jane from the beginning. They wanted her to do what she felt was right. They did not blame either Chuck or Jane for the pregnancy. They went to counseling sessions with Jane, and occasionally with Chuck.

Jane chose to have her baby and give it up for adoption. She said, "There is some guilt in giving our baby up, but neither of us is ready to cope with parenting. We're just kids ourselves."

Her schoolwork had suffered for the six weeks it took her to make the decision. Once Jane had made up her mind to give the baby up for adoption, her head was clear again and her schoolwork improved. She and Chuck continued to be friends, but their feelings had changed. They no longer dated.

Jane's school friends did not pay much attention to her pregnancy. Most of them treated her the same as ever. After all, there were other pregnant teenagers at school. However, Jane no longer went to movies or parties after school with her friends. As her pregnancy progressed, she no longer felt comfortable among others at school. It was all right in class, but during football games or at the mall she felt out of place.

Kathy

At fourteen, Kathy was shocked to find that she was pregnant. She was not ready for motherhood. She knew that for certain. Her boyfriend did not seem to share Kathy's worries about the future. Not that he did not care for her, but he seemed not to understand the seriousness of the situation.

Kathy had to make a decision. She felt very much alone. "I feel buried by decisions that need to be made, and I know that only I can make them. It's my life and my baby's life," she said.

Kathy was thinking about having an abortion. Deciding to end a pregnancy is very difficult. The abortion itself is usually not painful, but the decision to have one can be.

Many teenagers choose abortion, and they do so for good reasons. Kathy had seen a couple of girls in high school become mothers. They seemed worried about child care, money, work, and medical care. Kathy knew that was not the kind of life she wanted for herself and her baby. She wanted any baby of hers to have a good, solid start in life. She wanted financial security, love, and sharing for her children, and she knew she could not provide them for years to come. She could not count on her boyfriend to contribute anything.

She called a neighborhood teenage clinic and arranged for counseling. She had to skip band practice to get there, but had not had courage to tell her parents yet, so she couldn't ask her mother for a ride. It was very helpful to discuss abortion and her feelings about religion and life with the counselor at the clinic. She went back several times and talked to the counselor about values and about how her values related to her ideas about family, parenting, and education. Kathy came to realize that her entire life and her baby's life would be affected for years to come if she had the baby. She also had to face the fact that her boyfriend was not assuming responsibility for a situation he had helped to create. If she became a mother, it was clear she would be a single mother.

At the suggestion of the counselor, Kathy told her mother. They went to several counseling sessions together. They talked seriously about an abortion. The counselor explained that if this was Kathy's choice, she needed to make it soon. The safest and simplest method for abortion can be performed only in the earliest part of a pregnancy, before the third month is up. This is the *vacuum aspiration,* in which a tube is slid into the uterus through the vagina to vacuum out the embryo. It can be performed on an outpatient basis at a hospital or clinic with just a local anesthetic. It usually takes ten to fifteen minutes. Later in the pregnancy, abortion becomes more difficult and dangerous, and involves a hospital stay and an operation under general anesthetic.

The counselor wanted Kathy to understand that having an abortion was legal and that Kathy was the one who had to decide whether she wanted to have one or not. She thought hard for two weeks. She talked about it at home.

After a couple of weeks, Kathy had the abortion. Her mother drove her to the clinic. After the abortion, Kathy felt OK. Her mother drove her home right afterwards. She had some cramping and bleeding for about two weeks. She continued counseling for three more weeks and learned about the available contraceptive methods.

Kathy stayed in school. Sometimes she wondered what the baby might have been like. She felt wiser for the experience, but had no serious regrets. She had done what she felt best under the circumstances.

Franny and Gary

Franny had been dating Gary for four months. They were both fifteen and liked the outdoors, swimming, hiking, and biking. They were best friends and did everything together. But there was some tension in their friendship. When they kissed and hugged and occasionally petted, Franny wanted to go further. She wanted sex with more intensity than Gary did and that was creating some problems in their relationship.

Gary felt that the boy should take the initiative and

make decisions about when and how sexual intercourse would take place. The fact was, he loved kissing and hugging but did not want intercourse yet. He did not feel ready for that part of sex. This confused him. In his mind, the boy was supposed to chase the girl and demand sex—and here he was in a situation where just the opposite was true. What was wrong with him? He was evasive with Franny and sometimes even embarrassed.

Eventually he went to talk to a counselor at a teenage clinic. At first he was shy with Jack. But over a period of several weeks he learned to relax and to talk about himself. He learned to trust Jack not to laugh at the things he thought and felt. Finally, he confessed his dilemma to Jack. "I don't really want to have sex yet. Is that weird? Franny always wants to go all the way and I keep putting it off. She's going to think I'm a faggot or something."

Jack told Gary that different people have different internal clocks, and that important decisions such as when to have sexual intercourse should be made by listening to oneself, not one's friends or even one's girlfriend or boyfriend. Different people mature at different rates, both emotionally and physically. Some boys mature more slowly than girls the same age, and some girls mature more slowly than boys the same age.

Jack explained that many attractive and sexy boys and girls are really not ready for sexual intercourse, even when attractive partners are available and eager. Many teens have intercourse because they think it is expected of them—because it seems to be what everybody else is doing, in the movies and from the way they talk.

Jack helped Gary put it into words. "Do you want to go through life doing things others expect you to do? Or would you rather do what feels good and right for you?"

Gary eventually explained his feelings to Franny, with some hesitation. He felt he had to do it, for himself and for his relationship with Franny.

At first, Franny's feelings were hurt. She asked Gary if he was just "dumping" her. But Gary's sincerity and the closeness of their relationship finally convinced her that he was being honest with her and telling her the truth. They remained friends.

Chapter Seven
If You Think You're Pregnant

If you become pregnant, you might notice changes in your body right away. Your breasts might feel bigger and become a little sore. You might be sleepy much of the time. You might need to urinate more often. Some women feel sick to their stomach and may even throw up. Some notice a change in their sense of balance when they are exercising or working on dance or gymnastics. You might gain weight right away so that your clothes begin to feel a little tight.

However, you might not notice any signs of pregnancy at first. The only way your body indicates the changes going on may be by stopping your menstrual period. If you miss two periods, *go see a doctor*. Even if you have not noticed any other changes in the way you feel, you might be pregnant. Only a doctor can make the tests that will tell you for sure. If you wait, if you avoid the doctor and just hope that it's not true, you would miss the important early prenatal care. You might also run out of time to consider abortion as an option.

If the doctor says you are pregnant, you have an important decision to make. While you are thinking about it, be sure to follow your doctor's advice about nutrition, exercise, and general health. Even if you decide not to carry the baby the full nine months, you can keep yourself and the fetus healthier if you eat right and get the right exercise. If you do decide to have the baby, you will know you did what you could to make sure it was healthy—and that you stayed healthy too.

Once you know you are pregnant, you will need lots of information. If you are considering abortion, you may need to talk to a counselor to make sure this is what you want. You need advice about clinics and doctors. Check the resource list at the end of this book for places to find this information.

If you decide to have the baby, you will need information about pregnancy, childbirth, and your choices once the baby is born. The resource list at the end of this book is a good place to start.

If you want to keep the baby and raise it yourself, it's a good idea to start gathering information about caring for a baby as soon as possible. Some counseling services, schools, or family planning agencies offer classes in baby care, or they can refer you to places that do. And whether you decide to keep the baby or give it up for adoption, you should find out about everyone's legal rights and responsibilities. Your local Legal Aid Society or a legal services clinic can tell you, for example, what problems you might run into if you decide to try to raise your baby by yourself as a minor. In at least one state, the teenage father's parents have a financial responsibility for a teenage mother's baby. The legal services or adoption agencies that you look up in the yellow pages of the telephone directory can give you information about adoption. Family planning agencies or adoption agencies will offer counseling and tell you about the different types of adoption available.

Your school cannot force you to stay home or to join a special program for pregnant women. If you are pregnant and still living at home, you can get a home tutor or join a special program (if your school has one) or stay in your regular classes. If you stay in your regular classes, it may be difficult but you are more likely to keep up with your classmates and graduate on time.

If you do stay in high school and intend to graduate, you should make sure you know your school's policy on absence and lateness. Bring a note from your doctor or from home for every absence. Keep copies of your school report cards, especially if you are going to miss part of a term. Schools have been known to make mistakes on students' records, especially if the students have not been following the regular timetable. Your guidance counselor and school principal should be able to help you get the kind of schooling you want.

If you are too uncomfortable staying in school or if you can't stay at home until the baby is born, you can consider moving to a *group home* during your pregnancy. A social worker or guidance counselor will help you find a home that lets you continue your education. The resource list at the end of the book suggests other places to start looking for a group home.

What you decide to do about your pregnancy is your

decision, but it will affect your parents. Family planning agencies will respect your wishes about confidentiality. However, you will be most likely to be able to stay in school *and* keep the baby if you have the full support of your parents. Their financial help, their advice, and especially their baby-sitting time might make a big difference. Take them into consideration when talking to a counselor about your decision, or ask your parents to go to counseling with you.

If you think you're pregnant, the first thing you have to do is find out for sure. Then take it a step at a time. You have important decisions to make, but there are people who can help you think your way through them. There are places that offer information and advice. Use them.

WHERE TO GO FOR HELP

Organizations providing information and counseling about pregnancy, birth control, family planning, adoption:

Catholic Charities, 34 West 134th Street, New York, NY 10030 (Telephone: 212-281-9320). This is the New York service; check with your own archdiocese for similar services in your area.

Family Service Association of America, 44 East 23rd Street, New York, NY 10010 (Telephone: 212-674-6100)

Jewish Board of Family and Children's Services, 120 West 57th Street, New York, NY 10019 (Telephone: 212-582-6100)

The National Abortion Federation, 900 Pennsylvania Avenue, S.E., Washington, DC 20003. (Telephone: 800-223-0618 Monday-Friday, 10 A.M.-6 P.M. Eastern Standard Time)

The National Legal Aid and Defenders Association, 1625 K Street N.W., Washington, DC 20006 (Telephone: 202-452-0620). It can refer you to the local Legal Aid Society or Legal Services Corporation.

Planned Parenthood Federation of America, 810 Seventh
Avenue, New York, NY 10019, or your local chapter
(look in the phone book). Some centers do abortions, and any center can tell you where to get
contraceptive advice, prenatal care, adoption
counseling, or an abortion.

~#~

Local sources of help and information (try the Yellow
Pages of your telephone directory for specific phone num-
bers and addresses):

Adoption agencies
Day nurseries and child care centers
Legal services
Social service organizations (for group homes for preg-
nant women, counseling services, and more)
Your doctor (or look under "Physicians")
Your hospital or local clinic
Your clergy (minister, priest, rabbi)
Your local health department (look under the name of
your city, county, or state plus "Health Depart-
ment")

~#~

A few of the thousands of books available (ask at your
library or bookstore for more):

Atkinson, Linda. *Your Legal Rights.* New York: Franklin
Watts, 1982. Information about the legal rights
of minors.

The Boston Women's Health Book Collective. *The New Our Bodies Ourselves*. New York: Simon & Schuster, 1984. Covers women's health, conception and contraception, and sexuality.

Caplan, Frank, general editor. *The First Twelve Months of Life: Your Baby's Growth Month by Month*. New York: Bantam, 1978.

Kitzinger, Sheila. *The Complete Book of Pregnancy and Childbirth*. New York: Knopf, 1980.

Lindsay, Jeanne Warren. *Teens Parenting*. Buena Park, CA: Morning Glory Press, 1981.

Oettinger, Katherine, with Elizabeth C. Mooney. *Not My Daughter: Facing Up to Adolescent Pregnancy*. Englewood Cliffs, NJ: Prentice-Hall, 1979.

Richards, Arlene K. and Willis, Irene. *What To Do If You or Someone You Know Is Under Eighteen and Pregnant*. New York: Lothrop, Lee & Shepard Books, 1983.

Index